Birthing Purpose
21-Day
Devotional Journal

Bridgett McGill

The Queen Within LLC
Chicago, Illinois

Birthing Purpose 12-Day Devotional Journal Copyright ©2021

ISBN: 978-1-7367830-0-9

Published by The Queen Within LLC

For permission requests, contact Bridgett McGill at
thequeenwithin.org mcgillbridgett@gmail.com

Cover Designed by J. L. Woodson: www.woodsoncreative studio.com
Interior Designed by Lissa Woodson: www.Naleghnakai.com
Editor: Barbara J. Henry

Dedication

This journal is for every Beautiful and Divinely created WOMAN, who is gifted at birth with her purpose. No matter how long it takes her to see it, believe it and birth it – what she has inside her to bring forth is hers.

In the same way we can be pregnant physically, we can also be pregnant spiritually; with ideas, visions, inventions, projects, plans and the like. This 21-Day Birthing Purpose Journal is for you to discover, claim, put in writing, strategize, and give birth to your purpose. Your purpose, 'Oh Gifted One', is uniquely yours and no one can fulfill that purpose better than you.

As a community, we will be using this journal as a support in a 21-day corporate fast. During this 21-day fast, there is something for every single woman. If you want to birth a book, business, career change, education, love, self-love, grow your business, launch a non-profit, build higher self-esteem, become an entrepreneur and more, this is where your blueprint will be created.

A 21-Day fast is much easier to move through and complete with focus and support. This Interactive Journal can be used anytime you are ready to begin your birthing process. You will have access to daily meditations, mindfulness activities, self-care tools and more, to help you stay on track. And guess what? If at any point you falter, there's only one thing to do. You guessed it! Pick yourself up, dust yourself off, show yourself grace and compassion and jump back in.

Get Ready to Walk in Your Purpose!

Your Birthing Servant,

Queen Bea
Selah

Author's Note:

Unity with a group of women in a 21-Day Corporate Fast is where this project was born and has manifested into this 21-day Interactive Journal. Whenever you decide to complete a goal, the success is greater with intentional focus and support.

This journal was created with every woman in mind. The woman who loves deeply and the woman who needs to learn to love herself. It's for the woman who consistently pours out and the woman who needs pouring into. Some women love the verses of the bible, others prefer catchy quotes and smart phrases.

This is for the young woman trying to discover her life's purpose and for the mature woman who is taking her purpose to heights she's never reached.

Wherever you fall in this spectrum, you are included here; you have not been forgotten. We have all been gifted with a purpose and no two lives or purposes are the same. The year of Covid-19, forced many of us to pause. In that pause some women found themselves, or a self they hadn't been in touch with for a while. Some of us found our purpose, excelled in our purpose and honestly, many of us were just lost. That year is behind us; it's done, gone, over.

Please join us on this journey in the way that's best for you and together let's seek, find, invest in and give birth to our God-given purposes.

Your Birthing Purpose Servant,

Bridgett

Foreword

The 21-Day Fast; Birthed out of Science and Religion

The concept is simple enough; make a decision to be committed to a personal or professional goal for 21 consecutive days. After those three weeks, the pursuit of such goal could have developed into a new habit. Once you've established that habit, press in for another ninety days for it to become your lifestyle.

In the Bible, Daniel made a request of the king's guard that he and his fellow Hebrew brothers eat only vegetables and drink water, rather than dine on the delicacies from the King's table in Daniel 1:1-17. In Daniel 10:1-14 we find Daniel receiving dreams and revelations after his period of denial.

The brain is a super dope and complex organ; not quite a muscle that can contract or relax, but it does have the need to be made strong. We build our brain and keep it healthy by what we allow ourselves to receive. Dictionary on-line defines Neuroplasticity, as the brain's ability to respond to life and change itself by forging new neural pathways and circuits while pruning away old ones, as needed.

In layman's terms, this means if you change your mind, you change your life. A 21- Day fast of denial and focus on birthing your purpose can undoubtedly change the way you live.

MEDITATIONS:

For each of the 21 days, you have a meditation to focus on. These meditations haven't been written in any particular order, and each day references a spiritual, mental or physical birth. Take your time with each meditation. Sit with it, say it out loud, take a couple of deep breaths as you connect how it applies to you. It may apply to your life at this time, it may not. Meditation is another tool to guide you in focusing on and reaching your goals.

QUOTES / CHALLENGES:

These quotes have been selected because they give us added clarity in our thought process. We all have differences in what we subscribe to, and these quotes take us beyond religion. The challenges attached to each quote are exercises that have been scientifically proven in completing goals successfully.

SCRIPTURES / PRAYERS:

Everything we need to be successful in life can be found in the Word of God. The Bible is chock full of goals, purposes and prophecies that were completed and fulfilled. The scriptures and prayers included are written for those of us who believe in the power of The Most High God and the purposes and plans HE has for our lives.
Jeremiah 29:11 11 For I know the thoughts that I think toward you, saith the Lord, thoughts of peace, and not of evil, to give you an expected end..

ACCOUNTS OF MIRACULOUS BIRTHS:

The three births recorded here, although physical, are here to teach us spiritually. One or none of these accounts may apply to you now, but if you are a woman reading this, at some point, they will. If you are young, you have goals and purpose. If you are mature or in your golden years, you have goals and purpose. Sometimes we get in our own way; at other times that hindrance may be someone or something. Whatever the case may be, these three births prove to us that nothing can stop the plans and purposes of our lives. We need to be intentional about removing what's in the way ~ even if it's ourselves!

STRETCHES:

It's pretty common knowledge that when the mind, body and spirit work in unison, a person is able to show up as the best version of themselves. At times the "working" of the body can be convoluted in images of jogging, power walking, weight lifting and other aggressive exercises. The "stretch" should not be underestimated and be included in our daily bodily health and well-being. If for no other reason, stretching keeps us flexible, helps us to avoid stiffness and opens our lungs and muscles.

OILS:

The oils mentioned in this journal are special, useful, valuable and from the Earth. All essential pure oils are extracted from plants or trees directly from the ground. When essential oils are used in their purest form, the vast benefits and uses are amazing. Please make sure to experiment with 100% essential oils and not oil blends. All oils are not the same. Please be sure to read the labels of every bottle of oil to make sure it can be taken internally   ~Pour the Oil, My Sisters ~

CREATION IN NATURE:

The most marvelous, mystical and magical events occur in nature daily; hourly something new is birthed. In a world where creation is so natural, wouldn't it seem practical to spend some time in nature and let the magic infect us?

Each week you will be given an activity that will allow you to observe and experience the natural birthing process occurring in nature on a consistent basis. The Creator was in communication with mankind through nature, long before the written word. Humans were able to keep track of time with the sun, tell the seasons by nature's changing faces, and women kept track of their menstrual cycles and knew when they were with child by the moon. Use these activities to immerse yourself in the space where the birthing process is never ceasing.

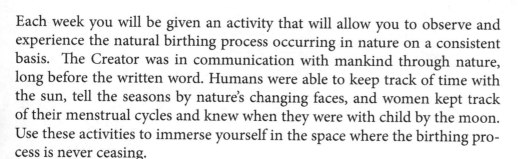

DETOX BATHS:

The definition of detox is to literally rid the body of poisonous substances. Those poisons, more often than not, show up in the woman's body as stress. A detox bath aids your body in eliminating toxins as well as absorbing the minerals and nutrients added to the water.

SPEAKER and SPEAKER NOTES:

Daily Testimonies are what you'll receive from 21 speakers for 21 days. Each of these women has a story, journey or message to share with you about the purposes they birthed out.

If you want to write a book, start a business, improve your finances, purchase real estate, lose weight and so much more, you are in the right place. At the end of each day, there is a journal section to write down notes from the Speaker of the Day. You will not want to miss a single testimony; they are all powerful and purposeful for such a time as this.

FASTING:

There are several variations of fasting. The goal of fasting is to deny yourself of something to open the pathway to receive something greater.

The fast associated with this journal is a 21-Day fast taken from the book of Daniel. It consists of consuming fruits, vegetables, beans, whole grains, nuts, water and tea only for 21 consecutive days.

Before you start any type of fast involving food restrictions, consult your physician; especially those of us who may be pregnant, have diabetes, struggles with hypoglycemia or any other medical conditions.

Be honest with yourself and choose a fast you can commit to, maintain and still have a level of denial. If you can't handle food restrictions, choose something else. A 21-day restriction of something you're used to will certainly be the challenge and sacrifice needed with intentional focus. Try fasting from one thing you enjoy; coffee, wine, alcohol, television, or social media. Whatever you decide, just know there's something greater waiting on the other side.

Meditation - Day 1

Write down anything and everything you ever dreamed of birthing, no matter how wild or outlandish it may be. Write as long as the ideas keep coming.

Ephesians 3:20 - Now to him who is able to do immeasurably more than all we ask or imagine, according to his power that is at work within us.

_____

_____

_____

_____

_____

_____

_____

_____

_____

_____

_____

Quote / Challenge - Day 1

"If you can't figure out your purpose, figure out your passion. For your passion will lead you right into your purpose."-- Bishop T.D. Jakes.

The Challenge today is three-part. The first part is to ask the question out loud . . .

Part one: "What is my Purpose?"

On the following journal lines, write the question nine times. Why nine? Because nine is the number of completeness of God and a symbol of finality. It also means that God completed his creation and all his promises. You are complete in your purpose. It is time to begin the activation of your purpose. Whatever ideas, projects, thoughts, visions come to your mind, write them all down. Don't stop writing until the thoughts stop. By writing the statement repeatedly, you activate the neuroplasticity in your brain. This helps to open up your thought channels.

Part two: Ask the question out loud,

"What are the things I'm passionate about?"

Write the question nine times as you did before. Record each and every passion as it comes to your mind.

Part three: On the following journal lines look at the purposes and the passions you recorded and see if you can match a purpose on line with a passion. Don't be surprised at how your purposes and your passions line up. They are both one in the same. Your purpose and passion are yours.

Day 1

SPEAKER NAME: _____

SPEAKER NOTES: _____

Meditation - Day 2

Turn back to ALL your birthing ideas from Day 1. For this day of Meditation, write down "I Can or I Will" in front of every single idea or thought you have. Add new thoughts and ideas if they come to mind.

Habakkuk 2:2 - "Write down the revelation and make it plain on tablets..."

_____

_____

_____

_____

_____

_____

_____

_____

_____

_____

_____

Scripture / Prayer – Day 2

Job 22:28

What you decide on will be done, and light will shine on your ways.

As you meditate on this scripture today, repeat this prayer. Write it down and record what it means to you. Let it be your prayer focus for today.

Father, you have given me Purpose to fulfill in my life. Those purposes were already within me at the time I entered this Earth. Let my feet follow the exact path you have given me to complete your decreed goals. Lord, if I fall off the path, I pray to remember to grab a hold of your amazing grace and tender mercies to lead me back to your great path. I thank you for the purposes and paths you have decided for me. I thank you for your light that will lead my way.

In the name of our Lord and Savior Jesus. Selah!

_____

_____

_____

_____

_____

_____

_____

_____

_____

Day 2

SPEAKER NAME: _____

SPEAKER NOTES: _____

_____

_____

_____

_____

_____

_____

_____

_____

_____

_____

_____

_____

Meditation - Day 3

Say a prayer to meet and be aligned with a Midwife to help you through your birthing process. She's waiting for you to make your request.

"What you seek is seeking you." - Rumi

_____

_____

_____

_____

_____

_____

_____

_____

_____

_____

_____

Miraculous Birth - Day 3
The Shunamite woman

When we open our Bibles to 2 Kings 4, starting in verse 8, we find the Shunamite Woman making a request of her husband to build a small room on the roof of their home, complete with furnishings. She wanted to provide a place of rest for the Man of God, Elisha, when he came to see them. This was no small feat.

We don't know her name, but we do know she is well-to-do. We also know she has been impacted by the Man of God's visits and has a husband who will bless her to bless others.

Elisha wanted to reward her kindness.

When the Man of God asked how he could he repay, she simply replied, "I have a home among my own people." Translation – "I'm good. I have everything I need. A husband, home, money, and status."

The Man of God, unsatisfied with her answer, inquired of his servant Gehazi, "What can we do for her?"

Gehazi had observed and noted with a few words, "Her husband is old and she has no son." In the conversations following, Elisha decreed she would have a child, not just bear a child, but a son, a legacy carrier, the following year at the same time. The woman was overwhelmingly distressed at his declaration. Why? Was she really good with all she had, or had she lost hope of the one thing she really wanted: an heir?

She did bear a son just as the Man of God said. The son was born; he grew, one day he had a headache, and he died. The Shunamite woman, accompanied by a servant, went in search of Elisha. She wanted to speak directly to the one who had decreed the promise, about what happened to the one who was decreed; her son.

Elisha came back to Shunem, and through Supernatural Touch, the boy was brought back to life.

What does this story teach us about dreams and goals? A few things. Her husband was old. We don't know if she was young or old. Was she past child bearing age? We don't know if she had conceived and miscarried. But what we do know is the specific notation of her husband being old. How old is old? Too old to produce sperm old; the bible doesn't tell us. The information we do have about the husband is one, he is busy. When the son complained of a headache, the husband gave the direction, "Take the boy to his mother." One, he didn't understand the reason for the urgency. The husband questioned why she had to go right away to see the man of God. The Bible gives no indication he even knew the boy was dead.

Sometimes the dreams and goals we have are blocked by others; intentionally or unintentionally. We are not always the one who is keeping us from our dreams or purpose. Who is in our space. What's the energy they are carrying? What mindset do they have about OUR goals that we may need to overcome?

Our dreams have to be protected. We may not be in position to leave a person or situation that is an obstacle to our dreams, goals, or purpose. But one thing is for sure and two for certain, dreams and goals can be protected by us mentally and spiritually. Be intentional about protecting your goals, dreams and purpose.

_____

_____

_____

_____

_____

_____

_____

_____

_____

_____

_____

_____

_____

_____

_____

Day 3

SPEAKER NAME: _____

SPEAKER NOTES: _____

_____

_____

_____

_____

_____

_____

_____

_____

_____

_____

_____

_____

_____

Meditation - Day 4

There are different Midwives for different births. If you need more than one Midwife, say a prayer for the Midwife you need for each purpose / project.

Example: The Midwife you need to birth a book is different from the Midwife you need to help you begin your Non-Profit.

_____

_____

_____

_____

_____

_____

_____

_____

_____

_____

_____

Stretch - Day 4

Forward fold – can be done standing, or supported. This stretch can also be done sitting in a chair, on the floor, and even in the bed.

Forward Fold stretch benefits:

- Stretches the hamstrings and back of calves.
- Strengthens the thighs and knees.
- Elongates the spine.
- Decreases stress, anxiety, depression, and fatigue.
- Calms the mind and relaxes the nerves.
- Relieves tension in the spine, neck, and lower back.
- Activates the abdominal muscles.

Forward fold is a restorative stretch that can aid in calming the autonomic nervous system and can help bring the energy down in the body, especially at bedtime. The forward fold can also soothe the nervous system and increase introspection. Finally, forward fold increases circulation to the nerves in the vertebrae of the spine.

Day 4

SPEAKER NAME: _____

SPEAKER NOTES: _____

_____

_____

_____

_____

_____

_____

_____

_____

_____

_____

_____

_____

_____

Meditation - Day 5

During your birthing process, be mindful of your circle. The wrong people around you could cause a stillbirth.

2 That Sanballat and Geshem sent unto me, saying, Come, let us meet together in some one of the villages in the plain of Ono. But they thought to do me mischief. --Nehemiah 6:2

_____

_____

_____

_____

_____

_____

_____

_____

_____

_____

_____

Bergamot: The Delicate Oil:

Bergamot oil is extracted from the rinds of Citrus Bergamia that grows on Bergamot orange trees. It is the most delicate of the citrus plants, requiring special climate and soil in order to thrive.

Bergamot is unique among citrus oils, possessing the duality of being both uplifting if you are sad, and calming, if you are anxious.

Bergamot has both topical and internal benefits.

It can be applied to the skin while showering and inhaled deeply to purify the skin and calm the mind. Adding a few drops to your facial cleanser purifies the delicate skin on the face.

Massaging the feet with bergamot and a carrier oil at bedtime aid in a good night's rest. This oil is frequently used in massage therapy.

For our tea drinkers, regular tea becomes Earl Grey tea by adding a few drops of Bergamot. In Greece, the unripe fruits are eaten by the spoonful as a dessert or with coffee. Recipes can be found through Google.

Other uses: Add a few drops to water in a diffuser for the classroom, at work, or at home when stress levels or tension is high.

As always, there may be some things to be mindful of. Depending on your skin, you may experience skin sensitivity.

All oils should be kept out of the reach of children.

If you are pregnant, nursing, or under a doctor's care, consult your physician. Avoid contact with eyes, inner ears, and sensitive areas. Avoid sunlight or UV rays for up to 12 hours after applying products.

Special note: all oils ARE NOT THE SAME. Please make sure to read ALL labels of oils you purchase. Because of the small amount of essential oils contained in some bottles, it may not be taken internally.

Day 5

SPEAKER NAME: _____

SPEAKER NOTES: _____

_____

_____

_____

_____

_____

_____

_____

_____

_____

_____

_____

_____

_____

_____

Meditation - Day 6

Conception / Pregnancy / Delivery! You cannot have one without the other, yet each part of birthing our purpose must be done in succession. Each step in the process has value; embrace every part.

"There is Purpose in the Process" – Bridgett McGill.

_____

_____

_____

_____

_____

_____

_____

_____

_____

_____

_____

Creation in Nature - Day 6

There's so much in nature that is born every single day. Today take a 10–30-minute walk. As you are walking, closely observe the plants, flowers, grass, trees. Let your meditative thought be this: "All things in nature grow naturally. The purpose I have is mine, so it shall manifest; naturally! I am preparing to receive and move in the natural flow and growth of my purpose."

_____

_____

_____

_____

_____

_____

_____

_____

_____

_____

_____

Day 6

SPEAKER NAME: _____

SPEAKER NOTES: _____

_____

_____

_____

_____

_____

_____

_____

_____

_____

_____

_____

_____

_____

Meditation - Day 7

The birthing process stops once you deliver (give birth). The mothering process then begins; it's time to care for, raise, nurture and protect your purpose/ project (baby).

_____

_____

_____

_____

_____

_____

_____

_____

_____

_____

_____

Detox Bath - Day 7

In a tub of water, add One 16oz box of baking soda, One 16oz bottle of peroxide and Two 8 oz cups of Epsom salt. Give yourself enough time to soak in the tub thirty minutes to one hour. If you have high blood pressure or blood pressure related issues, you can exchange the Epsom salt for Himalayan salt, Sea Salt or eliminate the salt altogether. Add to your relaxation by lighting a candle, using incense or playing some relaxing music.

_____

_____

_____

_____

_____

_____

_____

_____

_____

_____

_____

_____

Day 7

SPEAKER NAME: _____

SPEAKER NOTES: _____

_____

_____

_____

_____

_____

_____

_____

_____

_____

_____

_____

_____

_____

Meditation - Day 8

Are you pregnant with a baby (idea, project), but your fears, thoughts, lifestyle or habits may be stopping your birthing process? Be brutally honest in answering these questions below. This is your life and your purpose ~ your answers for your YOU!

_____

_____

_____

_____

_____

_____

_____

_____

_____

_____

_____

Quote / Challenge - Day 8

Quote: Maybe you've been assigned this mountain to show others it can be moved.--Unknown

Challenge:

Part of the reason this Interactive journal has been created is to guide women in birthing out their purpose. We have all been gifted with a purpose to fulfill, but sometimes we need direction, instruction or some other form of assistance to reach the end result.

*First re-read the quote.

*Next, think of a time that you were challenged to do something difficult and you did it!

*On the following journal lines, a) write down the challenge, b) write how you overcame it; did you devise a strategy? and c) what did it feel like when you had finished or (moved the mountain)?

*Bask in that moment. Give yourself a pat on the back or a big hug. Look in the mirror and with a great big smile say out loud

"GIRL, YOU DID THAT!"

Lastly: Think of your current purpose. What is the next goal you need to complete to get to your expected end? You've already proven to yourself you can move a mountain; so now let's move another.

Write the Purpose to be birthed out.

Plan and record the strategy in detail.

Give yourself a timeline or not.

And tomorrow give your Purpose (mountain) the first push. When you get distracted or discouraged, come back to your strategy. You may need to revise it, adjust it, or re-read it for a reminder. You have written your vision; you've made it plain, now start pushing.

Day 8

SPEAKER NAME: _____

SPEAKER NOTES: _____

_____

_____

_____

_____

_____

_____

_____

_____

_____

_____

_____

_____

_____

Meditation - Day 9

The Birthing process is your purpose. Only you can BIRTH what has been uniquely designed for you to birth.

The walls of the City of David had been torn down for 100+ years, yet Nehemiah rebuilt the wall in 52 days. The rebuilding of that wall was uniquely purposed for him.--Nehemiah 6:15

Scripture / Prayer – Day 9

John 16:21

A woman giving birth to a child has pain because her time has come; but when her baby is born, she forgets the anguish because of her joy that a child is born into the world.

As you meditate on this scripture today, repeat this prayer. Write it down and record what it means to you. Let it be your prayer focus for today.

El-Roi, we know you are as our sister Hagar describes you: "the One who sees us." Just as giving physical birth to a child is painful, my life's Purpose may be painful or hard at times. But Father, when Your purpose is fulfilled in me, my joy will be complete. I know Father, the Purposes you've given me are not just for me, but to bless the world around me. Let me bring forth my Purpose (baby) as you have decreed while I was still in my mother's womb.   Selah!

_____

_____

_____

_____

_____

_____

_____

_____

_____

Day 9

SPEAKER NAME: _____

SPEAKER NOTES: _____

_____

_____

_____

_____

_____

_____

_____

_____

_____

_____

_____

_____

_____

Meditation - Day 10

At times, the birthing process will require you to push past what you have been taught or what you've always known, and even break generational curses.

I was born breach and so was my daughter. Just because *we were born the same way* doesn't mean we will live the same life. ~ Kavata Robinson.

_____

_____

_____

_____

_____

_____

_____

_____

_____

_____

_____

Miraculous Birth - Day 10

David and Kate Ogg

On March 25, 2010, in Australia, Kate Ogg went into labor with her husband, Jim, by her side. They had been anxiously awaiting the arrival of their babies, conceived through invitro-fertilization.

After delivering the twins prematurely at 27 weeks, one of the twins, Jaime, was pronounced dead. Devastated, Jim and Kate were left in the room alone to say goodbye to their baby boy.

Kate had been holding Jaime against her bare chest for five minutes when she felt him move. The doctors came back into the room and wrote the movement off as nerve reflexes; not a sign of life. He was still dead THEY said.

Kate was still cuddling her son against her body when he opened his eyes. This prompted Kate to put some breast milk on her finger and into Jamie's mouth; his acceptance of the milk in true boy fashion was proof that he was alive.

Dreams delayed are not dreams denied. As much as we've heard this cliché phrase, do we believe it? What dreams and goals have died in our lives?

Just as baby Jaime was pronounced dead and was revived by the warmth, heartbeat and milk from his mother, your baby of purpose must be resurrected in the same way.

Day 10

SPEAKER NAME: _____

SPEAKER NOTES: _____

Meditation - Day 11

There may be an obstacle in our home or in a close relationship. We have to change our mindset, rather than our location, to complete the birthing process.

"What can be done for her?" Elisha asked. Gehazi said, "She has no son, and her husband is old." 2 Kings 4:14

_____

_____

_____

_____

_____

_____

_____

_____

_____

_____

_____

Stretch - Day 11

Tree pose is just the right pose to help create balance. The leg you're standing on is like the roots of your tree, and the stability in your pelvis carries energy from your roots, up into the spine and torso, creating a stronger core. The stretch goes deeper as you move your foot upward on your standing leg. With each movement, inhale and exhale into the leg that is bent for the greatest benefits of the stretch. The beauty in yoga is balance. Whatever you do to one side of the body, be sure to create balance by performing the stretch on the other side of the body as well.

Tree pose has many benefits:

- It strengthens the legs.
- It helps with balance and endurance.
- It improves alertness and concentration.

Day 11

SPEAKER NAME: _____

SPEAKER NOTES: _____

_____

_____

_____

_____

_____

_____

_____

_____

_____

_____

_____

_____

Meditation - Day 12

Just because we have a still birth does not mean we cannot birth another baby. The failing of one project doesn't mean you can't create/birth another.

I've failed over and over and over again in my life and that is why I succeed.
--Michael Jordan

_____

_____

_____

_____

_____

_____

_____

_____

_____

_____

_____

Oil - Day 12

Lavender oil: The Must Have oil.

Lavender is an essential oil derived from the lavender plant. Today, as well as in ancient times, people have used Lavender for bathing, relaxation, cooking, and as a perfume. It has qualities to calm and relax the mind and body. Lavender's versatile properties makes it the must have oil to have on hand at all times.

Topical and Internal uses:

Lavender is frequently used to reduce the appearance of skin imperfections. It is an excellent source of aromatherapy when added to bath water to soak away stress, or apply to the temples and back of the neck.

Add a few drops of Lavender to pillows, bedding, or bottoms of feet to relax and prepare for a restful night's sleep.

Take internally to help reduce anxious feelings.

Lavender can also be used in cooking to tone down citrus flavors and adds a flavorful twist to marinades, baked goods, and desserts.

Other uses:

Adding lavender to water in a spray bottle can be used to freshen your linen closet, car, or the air in your home or office. Adding three to four drops in a diffuser of choice creates a room full of aromatherapy.

As always, be mindful of skin sensitivity; try mixing the oil with a carrier oil should this occur.

All oils should be kept out of the reach of children.

If you are pregnant, nursing, or under a doctor's care, consult your physician. Avoid contact with eyes, inner ears, and sensitive areas. Avoid sunlight or UV rays for up to 12 hours after applying product.

Special note: all oils ARE NOT THE SAME. Please make sure to read ALL labels of oils you purchase. Because of the small amount of essential oils contained in some bottles, it may not be taken internally.

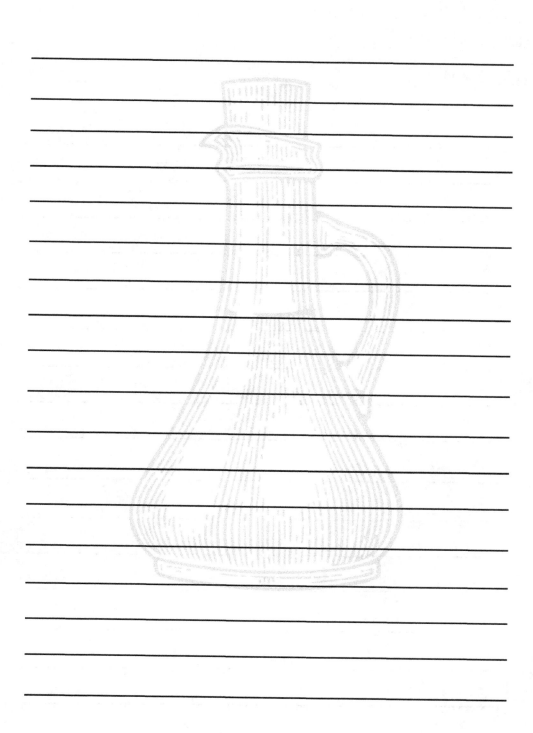

 *Day 12*

SPEAKER NAME: _____

SPEAKER NOTES: _____

_____

_____

_____

_____

_____

_____

_____

_____

_____

_____

_____

_____

_____

_____

Meditation - Day 13

When a baby (idea or project) dies, that does not mean we are no longer able to birth a new idea or project. Be intentional in leaving yourself open to get pregnant again (receive a new idea / project).

21 Then said his servants unto him, What thing is this that thou hast done? thou didst fast and weep for the child, while it was alive; but when the child was dead, thou didst rise and eat bread.

22 And he said, While the child was yet alive, I fasted and wept: for I said, Who can tell whether GOD will be gracious to me, that the child may live?

23 But now he is dead, wherefore should I fast? can I bring him back again? I shall go to him, but he shall not return to me.

24 And David comforted Bathsheba his wife, and went in unto her, and lay with her: and she bare a son, and he called his name Solomon: and the LORD loved him.

 2 Samuel 12: 21–24 KJV

_____

_____

_____

_____

_____

_____

_____

_____

_____

Creation in Nature - Day 13

Give yourself at least a 15-minute time frame today to take a ride. That ride can be by bicycle, scooter, motorcycle, car, or bus. No matter the choice of travel, take a ride and observe nature today. Admire the water along the lakefront, marvel at the trees in the park, observe people and how they fit in nature, and whether nature is fitting into them. You'll be surprised at how much you see on a nature ride. Have fun!

_____

_____

_____

_____

_____

_____

_____

_____

_____

_____

_____

Day 13

SPEAKER NAME: _____

SPEAKER NOTES: _____

_____

_____

_____

_____

_____

_____

_____

_____

_____

_____

_____

_____

_____

Meditation - Day 14

We are never too old to give birth to our baby (idea/project).

Luke 1:18 - Zacharias said to the angel, "How will I know this for certain? For I am an old man and my wife is advanced in years."

.

_____

_____

_____

_____

_____

_____

_____

_____

_____

_____

Detox Bath - Day 14

In a tub of water, add One cup Coconut Milk Powder, 1 cup Colloidal Oatmeal, 20 drops Lavender Essential Oil (optional). Give yourself enough time to soak in the tub thirty minutes to one hour. Add to your relaxation by lighting a candle or incense, or playing some relaxing music.

_____

_____

_____

_____

_____

_____

_____

_____

_____

_____

_____

Day 14

SPEAKER NAME: _____

SPEAKER NOTES: _____

_____

_____

_____

_____

_____

_____

_____

_____

_____

_____

_____

_____

Meditation - Day 15

No matter how young we may be when we become pregnant with an idea, vision or project, youth is not a determining factor of the birthing process.

1 Timothy 4:12 - Don't let anyone look down on you because you are young, but set an example for the believers in speech, in conduct, in love, in faith and in purity.

_____

_____

_____

_____

_____

_____

_____

_____

_____

_____

_____

_____

Quote / Challenge - Day 15

Quote: The Purpose of Life, is a Life of Purpose.

Robert Byrne

Challenge: In the next 24-hours, Write or Speak your next Purpose to be fulfilled 100x. There is much science behind the 100x method. Some of that Science includes you being able to see your progress, and it increases your thought process about a goal to be accomplished.

Write 100x: I will fulfill my purpose to _____.

Speak Out Loud 100x: I will fulfill my purpose to_____.

Mix it up: Write it 50x and Speak it 50x.   It's all up to you!

_____

_____

_____

_____

_____

_____

Day 15

SPEAKER NAME: _____

SPEAKER NOTES: _____

_____

_____

_____

_____

_____

_____

_____

_____

_____

_____

_____

_____

Meditation - Day 16

Distractions deny us of our destiny. We must stay focused!
Take a moment and listen to the words of the song by Kevin Levar titled "Your Destiny."

_____

_____

_____

_____

_____

_____

_____

_____

_____

_____

_____

_____

Scripture / Prayer ~ Day 16

Psalm 57:2 I cry out to God Most High, to God who will fulfill his purpose for me. New Living Translation

As you meditate on this scripture today, repeat this prayer. Write it down and record what it means to you. Let it be your prayer focus for today.

Jehovah-Shalom, I pray the purposes that manifest in my mind that I believe are mine, will be in alignment with the purposes you have for me. Lord I desire to live in your will in the midst of, because of and in spite of. I pray what you desire for me, Most High God, would be what I desire for myself. There is nothing missing, lacking or broken in my life because of the purpose you have set before me to fulfill.   Selah!

_____

_____

_____

_____

_____

_____

_____

_____

_____

Day 16

SPEAKER NAME: _____

SPEAKER NOTES: _____

_____

_____

_____

_____

_____

_____

_____

_____

_____

_____

_____

_____

Meditation - Day 17

Whatever purpose you birth into the earth will bless the world around you.

Samuel 1:11 And she made a vow, saying, "LORD Almighty, if you will only look on your servant's misery and remember me, and not forget your servant but give her a son, then I will give him to the LORD for all the days of his life, and no razor will ever be used on his head." --Hannah

_____

_____

_____

_____

_____

_____

_____

_____

_____

_____

Miraculous Birth - Day 17

Sarah, the wife of Abraham, giving birth to her first child at the age of 90, was miraculous indeed. But not to the Creator, who deemed it so. Every woman is born into the earth with all the eggs in her body she will ever have. This means Sarah came to this earth with Isaac in her womb. When she bore her first child, again, at the age of 90, it was her birthright plan: to be Isaac's mother. The Isaac who the Most High said he would have a covenant with. Sarah then can also be known as the Mother to the Son of Covenant.

The story of Sarah teaches us two very important lessons: One, no matter how old we are, if there is a purpose for us to complete, we can complete it. If there's an assignment on our lives, that assignment is ours, with no age requirement.

Secondly, Sarah teaches us there is no circumventing our purpose. She pushed Abraham to sleep with her maidservant, Hagar, and impregnate her in an attempt to fulfill the promise; she was out of order. The assignment for her to birth the leader of nations was hers, not Hagar's. The Lord in HIS graciousness didn't forget about Ishmael and blessed him greatly too "but…." The Lord said, HIS covenant would be with Isaac.

Just as we are never too young to live out our purpose, assuredly, we are never too old. Don't let age and the passing of time interrupt or stop what you were purposed to do at birth.

_____

_____

_____

_____

_____

_____

_____

Day 17

SPEAKER NAME: _____

SPEAKER NOTES: _____

_____

_____

_____

_____

_____

_____

_____

_____

_____

_____

_____

_____

Meditation - Day 18

There is nothing new under the sun. Whatever you have been blessed to birth out in purpose, it is for you to birth. Don't worry about the woman who has the same idea or business as you; there is nothing new under the sun. The way you birth out your purpose will be like no one else!

Ecclesiastes 1:9 ~ What has been will be again, what has been done will be done again; there is nothing new under the sun.

_____

_____

_____

_____

_____

_____

_____

_____

_____

_____

_____

Stretch - Day 18

Laying on your back with your feet against the wall is a restorative stretch. This stretch can be done on the floor or in your bed, again, with your feet up the wall and with your backside as close to the wall as possible.

- Elevating the legs promotes drainage from excess fluid build-up. In addition, gravity assists circulation by facilitating the return of blood back to the heart.

- Soothes swollen or cramped feet and legs.

- Legs against the wall has been known to be a treatment for reducing swelling and pain in the lower extremities.

- Relieves lower back tension.

_____

_____

_____

_____

_____

_____

_____

_____

_____

_____

Day 18

SPEAKER NAME: _____

SPEAKER NOTES: _____

_____

_____

_____

_____

_____

_____

_____

_____

_____

_____

_____

_____

Meditation - Day 19

When we intentionally make the decision to commit Spiritual Abortion, we have decided we can't, we won't, we don't want to figure it out. Our purpose is tied to our destiny. Think very carefully before you completely give up. Your destiny and everything attached to your destiny is lost when you make the decision to quit.

_____

_____

_____

_____

_____

_____

_____

_____

_____

_____

_____

Oil - Day 19

Myrhh: The Valuable oil.

This highly valued essential oil is derived from the sacred gummy resin of the small, thorny Myrrh tree. These trees are almost impossible to grow outside of the Arabian Peninsula. Today, in the 21st Century, this oil is constantly in short supply and high demand.

Ancient records show that Myrrh was deemed so valuable that at times it was valued at its weight in gold and has been used for centuries for its internal and external health benefits. Myrrh has been used throughout history as a perfume, incense, and health aid. It was also employed in embalming and religious ceremonies.

Topical and internal uses:

Myrrh has powerful cleansing properties, especially for the mouth and throat. Add one to two drops to a couple ounces of water and gargle for a quick mouth rinse. Adding one to two drops to toothpaste gives added cleansing to the mouth, teeth and gums.

It is also soothing to the skin when applied topically—promoting a smooth, youthful-looking complexion. Adding three to four drops to your lotion/moisturizer helps reduce the appearance of fine lines and wrinkles.

Other uses:
Add two to four drops to a diffuser to create a balanced atmosphere.

All oils should be kept out of the reach of children.

If you are pregnant, nursing, or under a doctor's care, consult your physician. Avoid contact with eyes, inner ears, and sensitive areas.

Special note: all oils ARE NOT THE SAME. Please make sure to read ALL labels of oils you purchase. Because of the small amount of essential oils contained in some bottles, it may not be taken internally.

Day 19

SPEAKER NAME: _____

SPEAKER NOTES: _____

_____

_____

_____

_____

_____

_____

_____

_____

_____

_____

_____

_____

_____

_____

Meditation - Day 20

Birthing out our purpose comes with a peace like no other. Because it's your birthright, completing your purpose is destiny fulfilled.

"The two most important days in your life are the day you are born and the day you find out why." – Mark Twain.

_____

_____

_____

_____

_____

_____

_____

_____

_____

_____

_____

United with Nature - Day 20

Today the goal is to be united with nature. If it's possible, sit or walk in the grass, dirt or sand; this is called grounding. The earth pulls toxins from your body during this process.

If this is not quite your forte', try sitting in the grass on a blanket or in a chair. Whatever position you decide on, close your eyes, allow yourself to inhale and exhale deeply for at least fifteen minutes and become one with nature. Imagine yourself as part of a tree, a blade of grass or an animal in nature. EnJoy!

_____

_____

_____

_____

_____

_____

_____

_____

_____

_____

_____

Day 20

SPEAKER NAME: _____

SPEAKER NOTES: _____

_____

_____

_____

_____

_____

_____

_____

_____

_____

_____

_____

_____

_____

Meditation - Day 21

You are Worthy of completing your Birthing process. Whatever has been placed inside you by the Creator to birth out is YOUR BABY! No one can do it like you and no one is going to do it like you are going to do it. Your baby will be brought to life when you believe and take action on that belief.

_____

_____

_____

_____

_____

_____

_____

_____

_____

_____

_____

Detox Bath - Day 21

In a tub of water, add One cup of Epsom salt, ½ cup of baking soda, 3 drops of Eucalyptus essential oil, 8 drops vanilla in jojoba oil. Give yourself enough time to soak in the tub thirty minutes to one hour. Add to your relaxation by lighting a candle, using incense or playing some relaxing music.

_____

_____

_____

_____

_____

_____

_____

_____

_____

_____

_____

Day 21

SPEAKER NAME: _____

SPEAKER NOTES: _____

_____

_____

_____

_____

_____

_____

_____

_____

_____

_____

_____

_____

_____

Day 21:

ARE YOU READY TO PUSH OUT YOUR PURPOSE?

_____

_____

_____

_____

_____

_____

_____

_____

_____

_____

_____

_____

_____

Acknowledgements

I used to think the saying 'Giving Glory and Honor to the Most High God who is the head of my life' was so cliché. As I live and move in my daily walk with the Creator, this statement has never been so real to me as it is in this time of my life. I give ALL praises to the Creator, who allowed me to be birthed into the earth to Robert and Demetry. HE blessed me to give birth and allowed me to see the birth of my Children's children. All Glory is truly due to HIM.

Along this path I have been blessed beyond words to meet, connect with, break bread with, love on and be loved by, some of HIS treasured possessions – Women. I give thanks to every Queen who has ever encouraged me, corrected me, prayed for or with me and stood with me in my mountain top highs and mud digging lows.

My Daughter-Queens, Kwaanza Andenisha, Kayla Ayomide Omotola and the seed of my seed, Zora Kartier, have taught me how to live above the noise and be still in the chaos.

To my cousin Khaleelah, what a ride it's been. I'm so grateful for your constant push, corrections, challenges, prayers and the constant laughter that has helped me overcome many struggles. You are the best!

To Kelly Mahomes, a woman whose love for The Most High God has moved me to many tears, over many years. You are so valuable to God and HIS Kingdom. I am always intentional in seeking your wisdom and input for my projects. You are solid and filled with HIS HOLY SPIRIT, my sister/friend.

With Gratitude, I love you all deeply.

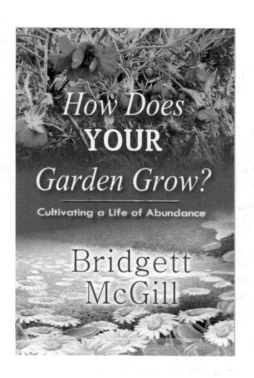

If you compared your life to a garden right now, right today, what would you find? Is it flourishing, lush and full; are there a few green spots here and some brown patches there, or is it depleted because you've given everything away? We have to ask ourselves every day; What does my garden need? Does it need the sun of encouragement; could it benefit from the fertilizer of forgiveness; would the pruning of confession bring great relief, or is it simply craving the beauty of rest?

As we walk through the gardens of our lives, we will find that we have within us all we need to cultivate a life of abundance; we only have to be still, listen and let the beauty come forth.

~~~~~~
~~~~~~
~~~~~~~~~~~~~~~~~~~~~~~~~~~~~~~~~~~~~

How Does Your Garden Grow? Cultivating a Life of Abundance, Interactive Journal is an amazing tool to cultivate growth and healing. In this interactive journal, you will go beyond writing "What are you thinking and what are you feeling." This journal will challenge you to dig into your heart, pull up weeds of stagnation, fertilize your desires and sow into your creativity. This workbook, if you will, is filled with questions, challenges, prayers quotes, scriptural references for further biblical study and excerpts from the book *"How Does Your Garden Grow? Cultivating a Life of Abundance* by Bridgett McGill

REDEMPTION

BRIDGETT MCGILL

Khalil Benson has taken on the biggest case of his legal career. His client pulled the trigger, but something else might be the cause of the victim's death. Pressure mounts as the media and public press for answers in a city cover-up. Khalil will need his street savvy gained from growing up on Chicago's westside, and his experience winning cases and that others considered lost causes, and a dedicated team, to unravel the threads of secrecy and betrayal to bring down a politically connected prosecutor and free his client.

Ava Penwood has settled in for the long haul after serving three of a thirty-five-year sentence, the aftermath of a night out that went horribly wrong. Until hope, packaged as a legal hotshot who has come into startling new information about her case, walks in with the promise of an appeal. Now she has to wrestle with her growing attraction for a man she barely knows and holds the balance of her life in his hands.

Facts or Fate ... what will be true Redemption?

Bridgett McGill

is the award-winning author of *How Does Your Garden Grow? Cultivating a Life of Abundance*, released in 2017. This inspirational book has an accompanying Interactive Journal. Her latest journal, *Birthing Purpose*, releases summer 2021. She will release her first novel *Redemption*, fall, 2021

Bridgett is an Elementary Education teacher. She is also a certified yoga instructor with ACT yoga and practices daily to clear her mind and increase her creative flow.

Affectionately known as "Ms. Bridgett," she lives in Chicago and is the mother of two adult daughters and a beautiful granddaughter.

CPSIA information can be obtained
at www.ICGtesting.com
Printed in the USA
LVHW011107100921
697539LV00018B/977